# SNOWBOARDING

## A COMPLETE GUIDE FOR BEGINNERS

### GEORGE SULLIVAN

ILLUSTRATED WITH PHOTOGRAPHS

PUFFIN BOOKS

ACKNOWLEDGMENTS

Special thanks are offered photographer Jerry LeBlond of Rutland, Vermont, for his skill and excellence in taking the instruction photographs that appear in the book. Special thanks are also due Bob Evegan, Snowboard Instructor, Killington Resort, Killington, Vermont, for providing his expertise at the picture-taking sessions, and Dana Hackett, who posed for the photos.

The author is also very grateful to the many snowboarding specialists and experts who provided information and advice in the preparation of this book, and read sections of the manuscript for accuracy. These include Sarah Hathaway and Emmet Manning, Burton Snowboards, Burlington, Vermont; Tom Myers, Vermont Ski Areas Association; John Ingersoll, Director, High Cascade Snowboard Camp, Bend, Oregon; Gina Bertucci, Camelback Ski Area, Tannersville, Pennsylvania; Susie Barnett-Bushong, Grand Targhee Ski Resort, Alta, Wyoming; and Doug Werner, author of *Snowboarders Start-Up!* The author was also aided and supported by webmaster Don Wigal (www.wigal.com); Ellen LiBretto, Queensboro Public Library; Aime LaMontagne, Jr.; and Dick Darnell.

Cover photographs courtesy of Burton Snowboards. Front: Jeff Curtes (photographer), Nicole Angelrath (rider). Back, left to right: Jeff Curtes (photographer), Terje Haakonsen (rider), Jeff Curtes (photographer), Jason Brown (rider); Vianney Tisseau (photographer), Nicole Angelrath (rider).

PHOTOGRAPH CREDITS

Burton Snowboards, 12 (both), 15 (both), 16 (both), 32; by Jeff Curtes, 4, 36, 41; by Vianney Tisseau, 8, 33; by David Urban, 18. High Cascade Snowboard Camp, 9, 35, 38, 39; Jerry LeBlond, 10, 20 (both), 23, 24 (both), 25 (both), 27 (both), 28 (both), 30 (all), 31 (all), 43 (both); George Sullivan, 6.

PUFFIN BOOKS
Penguin Books USA Inc., 375 Hudson Street, New York, New York 10014, U.S.A

First published in the United States of America by Cobblehill Books, an affiliate of Dutton Children's Books, a division of Penguin Books USA Inc., 1997
Published simultaneously in Puffin Books

10 9 8 7 6 5 4 3 2 1

The Library of Congress has cataloged the Cobblehill edition as follows:
Sullivan, George.
Snowboarding ; a complete guide for beginners / George Sullivan :
illustrated with photographs.    p.    cm.
ISBN 0-525-65235-3
1. Snowboarding. I. Title. GV857.S57S87 1997
796.9—dc20 96–22756 CIP AC

Puffin Books ISBN 0-14-056181-1

Printed in Hong Kong

# CONTENTS

In terms of excitement and thrills, few sports can equal snowboarding. This is Nicole Angelrath, a member of the professional team sponsored by Burton Snowboards.

# 1. HOT SPORT IN A COLD SEASON

*"IT'S A GREAT SPORT,"* says one enthusiast. "It's as close to flying as you can get."

That's snowboarding, a sport that includes many of the features of surfing and skateboarding. It's something like skiing, too.

The snowboard itself is a fiberglass, metal-edged board that is several feet in length and looks something like an extra-wide ski. Plastic or metal bindings hold your boots to the board.

After stepping into the bindings, you are standing sideways to your direction of travel (like a surfer). You face forward and bend your knees. Once you're gliding down a hill, you use your toes and heels to pressure the board's edges to change direction and stop.

As a skilled rider, you'll enjoy the thrills and excitement of sweeping down a mountainside or twisting and flipping your way over the jumps, rails, and banks of a snowboard park.

Some people say that snowboarding is on its way to becoming the nation's No. 1 mountain sport. Still, it's a relatively new sport, having gotten started as recently as 1963. That's the year that young Tom Sims of Haddonfield, New Jersey, crafted a 30-inch plywood snowboard in his eighth-grade shop class. He called it a skiboard. Sims later formed a company that became one of the leading manufacturers of snowboards.

In 1965, Sherman Poppen bolted two wood skis together side-by-side to create another early version of the snowboard. It looked like a very wide ski. Called the Snurfer, Poppen's invention had a

*All but a small handful of ski areas now offer trails especially for snowboarders.*

rope attached to the nose which the rider grasped for balance and to help steer. Steel tacks poked up through the Snurfer's deck to hold the rider's boots in place.

Poppen organized Snurfer races at Blockhouse Hill near Muskegan, Michigan. For most contestants, the biggest challenge didn't come from other racers but just from being able to finish with the board under one's feet. Only about half of the riders were able to do so.

In 1979, after more than a decade of Snurfer competition, 25-year-old Jake Burton Carpenter showed up at Blockhouse Hill with a fiberglass board that resembled a surfboard. It featured bindings that made board control much easier. Organizers of the event were ready to turn Jake away, claiming their contest was only for Snurfers. They compromised by creating an "open division" for Jake and his Burton Snowboard.

Jake Burton Carpenter didn't merely invent a practical snowboard. He created an industry. More than one hundred companies manufacture snowboards today. Burton Snowboards, with its headquarters in Vermont, is No. 1 in snowboard sales.

During the decade of the 1980s, the modern

snowboard, with its polyethylene base and steel edges, came into existence. High-back bindings were also introduced. These made it possible to control a board even on hard-packed snow. Soft boots were another innovation.

In 1982, national snowboarding championships were held for the first time and the following year the world championships were introduced. Europeans began to organize snowboard competition in 1986.

Despite the technical advances and snowboarding's booming popularity, skiers and the ski industry in general resisted the sport for years. Only a few of the country's more than 500 mountain resorts would accept boarders at first, considering them rowdy and reckless.

Snowboarding continued to struggle for acceptance through most of the 1980s. As the numbers of boarders kept doubling and redoubling, attitudes changed. By the early 1990s, all but a small handful of ski areas had the welcome mat out for snowboarders. Snowboarding had become "undisputed king of the mountain," said The New York Times.

Further evidence of the sport's wide approval came late in 1995 when it was announced that snowboarding would be making its debut as an Olympic sport in 1998. In Olympic competition, medals are awarded in men's and women's freestyle and giant slalom. (The slalom is a race against the clock over a zigzag course laid out around flag-topped poles.)

By 1996, there were slightly more than two million snowboarders, according to the National Sporting Goods Association. It's estimated there will be close to four million by 2000.

In Canada, snowboarding has enjoyed the same mushrooming growth. By 1996, Canada could boast more than 3,000 certified snowboard instructors. Competition in the sport was being held on a regional, provincial, and national basis. For snowboarders, many mountain resorts carefully construct half-moon shaped furrows in the snow called "halfpipes" or offer special parks with specially built terrain. You can rent snowboards, boots, and other equipment and there are snowboard clinics or schools —"boarding schools"— where beginners can learn the fundamental skills after a few lessons and a couple of days of practice.

*Burton's Johan Olofsson flies high over a halfpipe
in the Swiss Alps.*

Of course, snowboarding isn't limited to ski areas. You can snowboard about anywhere there's sloping terrain and three or four inches of snow. It's estimated that about 30 percent of all boarders pursue the sport on back hills, never visiting a ski area.

You won't be snowboarding for very long before you notice there's a big difference between boarding and other sports. In skiing or ice skating, in bowling or trying to hit a baseball, there's a right way and a wrong way for doing it. In snowboarding, it's different. While there are certain basics that apply, it's a sport that encourages you to be expressive, to develop your own style. Snowboarding stresses creativity.

There's one other feature that makes snowboarding unique. Skiing came into existence as a form of transportation. The same is true of ice skating. Basketball, football, and soccer and many other sports were originated for competition. Not snowboarding. The whole idea in snowboarding is to have fun.

"Hey, dude, let's go boarding!"

# 2. TAKING LESSONS

*TAKING LESSONS* is the easiest way to learn snowboarding. Most ski areas have special schools or clinics for beginners. At a school, you're likely to make progress much faster than if you simply try to work things out by yourself.

In a typical group lesson, it's likely that your class will be made up of four to eight beginners. After some stretching exercises and a talk on safety, you'll do some drills that will help you to get used to the feel of the board.

Next, you'll work on balancing and gliding on the board in a straight line for a short distance. On a gentle slope, you'll practice edging, sideslipping, traversing, and turning.

Inquire about lesson packages at mountain resorts in your area. These include equipment

*Summertime campers at the High Cascade Snowboard Camp pose for their class photo.*

9

*Fourteen-year-old Dana Hackett, who posed for many of the instruction photographs in this book, with Bob Evegan of the Killington Resort, Killington, Vermont, a member of the Professional Ski Instructors of America.*

A number of mountain resorts in the West and on the Pacific Coast offer summertime camps for boarders. At the High Cascade Snowboard Camp, near Bend, Oregon, where you ride Mount Hood's high-mountain summer snowfield, the program is tailored to your level of experience. "Riders — age 10 and above — are grouped according to their riding interest and ability," says camp director John Ingersoll. "Mornings are spent riding with your coach, learning new skills and tricks. In the afternoon, you choose the pro you want to ride with and decide what skills or tricks you want to learn, like freeriding, halfpipe transitions, flat-land tricks, spin tricks."

At the Grand Targhee Ski and Summer Resort in Alta, Wyoming, the snowboard camp is directed by Mike Jacoby, a member of the U.S. Snowboard Team.

Snowboarding magazines often carry the names and addresses of such camps. Call or write those that interest you for information as to schedules and rates. A local ski shop is also likely to have such information.

rental as well as instruction in snowboarding's basics.

# 3. CHOOSING A BOARD

*SNOWBOARDS* are turned out in so many varieties, it may seem that there are no two alike. But if you take your time and get some advice, you'll find a board to suit your size, sex, level of experience, and boarding style.

In manufacturing snowboards, the most common method is to use laminated sheets of fiberglass molded over a wooden core. The board is then fitted with metal edges and a polyethylene base. These materials can vary widely in quality.

The board also includes threaded inserts into which the bindings are mounted. The average board costs from $250 to $500.

Board length and width are stated in centimeters. (2 1/2 centimeters are about equal to 1 inch; 30 centimeters are about equal to one foot.) Boards range in length from 100 to 200 centimeters (from 3 feet, 3 inches, to 6 feet, 6 inches). They're from 15 to 30 centimeters (6 to 12 inches) in width. They weigh from 5 to 10 pounds.

Several factors should be considered in choosing a board. Your height and weight are important. Generally speaking, taller and heavier riders require a board that has greater running length and more edge contact than average. In choosing a board that's the right size, one rule of thumb says to stand the board in front of you, heel down; the tip should come to somewhere between your chin and nose.

But this advice doesn't always apply. It's a good

*Freestyle/freeride board with identical nose and tail.*

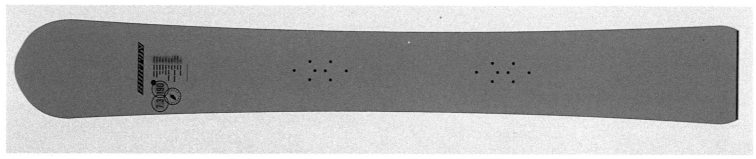

*Alpine boards are narrow and fast. Note the sidecut.*

idea to visit a snowboard shop to get more information. A snowboard instructor at a ski area can also be helpful.

Boards also vary in the amount of flexibility they have. A board that is more flexible than average is said to be "softer." A board with less flexibility is termed "stiff."

Sidecut is another characteristic that boards

have. Place a board on one of its edges on a flat surface and notice the gap between the edge itself and the surface. The board's tip and tail are wider than the waist; the board has an hourglass shape.

Sidecut is an important factor in determining how a board will ride. With little sidecut, a board is more likely to slide through a turn. With lots of sidecut, there's more of a tendency for the board's edges to slice through the snow when turning, that is, to carve. Every rider wants to carve.

Snowboard manufacturers offer two basic kinds of boards: freestyle/freeride and alpine. Freestyle/freeride boards are recommended for most beginners. They are generally shorter in length, softer, and have less sidecut. These characteristics make the board easier to maneuver. A freestyle/freeride board may be just what you need for relaxed cruising in soft snow.

Some freestyle/freeride boards are also twin-tipped, that is, the shape of the tip and tail are identical. This feature allows such boards to be ridden backward as well as forward. As this sug-gests, freestyle boards are well-suited for trick riding.

Alpine boards have a longer running length than freestyle/freeride boards. They're also nar-rower and stiffer. The greater length, flexibility, and sidecut of an alpine board impart increased sta-bility at higher speeds. For ripping down a moun-tain, executing perfectly carved turns on even the hardest snow pack, the alpine board is what's preferred. It is also the board that racers choose.

It's a good idea to rent a demonstration board and the other equipment the sport requires before you buy. Most areas have rental shops where you can obtain a board, boots, and bindings. A good feature of the rental shop is that it is likely to be staffed by trained personnel who will help to assure that the board you choose is suitable for your size and boarding experience.

Renting, however, can be costly, requiring a sizeable deposit. To cut your costs, deal with a shop that will allow you to apply your rental charges toward your purchase. Or look for end-of-the-sea-son sales or consider buying used equipment.

# 4. BOOTS AND BINDINGS

*GETTING BOOTS* that fit right is vital. Your boots, which buckle into bindings on the board, are what transfer your energy to the board's edges in turning.

For years, women riders had to make do with men's boots, which hindered them on the slopes. (Women generally have slimmer heels and higher arches than men.) But during the mid-1990s, Burton and a handful of other manufacturers began to offer boots especially for women. They're now available everywhere.

In snowboarding, there are soft boots and hard boots. Most young snowboarders choose soft boots. They're light in weight and yet provide the support you need.

Most soft boots have two parts—a flexible outer boot with a treaded sole, an inner bladder that fits to the contour of your foot, providing support and holding the heel in place.

Hard boots are similar to skier's boots and are stiffer and heavier than soft boots. They also have inner bladders.

Soft boots generally go with freestyle/freeride boards. Hard boots, which give greater edge control, are favored by racers and alpine boarders. They are often the choice of skiers who take up snowboarding.

Bindings are what hold your boots to the board. One big difference between snowboard bindings and those used in skiing is that snowboard bindings don't release during a fall, as skiers' bindings do.

*Soft boots are worn by most riders, especially beginners.*

*Hard boots are favored by racers and one-time skiers.*

With soft boots, you'll want bindings that offer a high-back molded plastic heel cup to support the ankle. Straps with adjustable buckles secure the boots on the board.

Plate bindings are used with hard boots. They tightly clamp the boots in place. Some types offer a disc-shaped plate that allows the rider to easily adjust the angle of his or her stance.

You determine the placement of the bindings to suit the width of your stance and angle them to suit your boarding style. The snowboard's threaded inserts permit the bindings to be easily mounted to the board's surface.

Generally, the rear binding is placed at right angles to the board. The front binding is angled slightly forward.

Keep in mind that once you've decided on the width and angle of your stance, the decision isn't etched in stone. You can change the placement of the bindings if your stance doesn't feel right.

Besides boots and bindings, you also need a safety strap. This is a strap that connects your front leg to the front binding. When you're on any kind of an incline, and buckling on your boots, the safety strap prevents your board from escap-

*Bindings for soft boots feature a plastic heel cup and adjustable straps.*

*Step-in plate bindings clamp hard boots in place. This style offers an adjustable disc plate used in fixing stance angle.*

ing and zooming down the hill. Many areas require the use of a safety strap.

Also get a deck mat, a small piece of nonskid material that attaches to the board in-between the bindings. It provides traction for your back foot when it is out of its binding, as when you're skating or riding a lift.

Once you own your own equipment, get familiar with it at home. Put on your boots, place the board on the carpet, then strap in both feet. Stand upright, bend your knees. Practice shifting your weight from one foot to the other, that is, from front to back.

Practice edging, an important skill. To achieve a toe edge, roll your weight onto the balls of your feet and pressure the edge of the board into the carpet. Roll your weight onto your heels for a heel edge.

A couple of practice sessions at home won't take more than a few minutes or so, yet they'll make you a more confident boarder as you head for the slopes for the first time.

# 5. WHAT TO WEAR

*WHEN SELECTING CLOTHING* for a sport like snowboarding, think in terms of layers. Several layers of light, close-fitting clothing produce much greater warmth than a single heavier garment.

And layered clothing can be easily adapted to the day's temperature. If it warms up, you can take off a sweater. If it turns colder, you can add one.

Your outer jacket and pants should be windproof and waterproof. As a beginner, you're going to spend a good amount of time sitting in the snow. It's not just from falling down, but you have to sit down to adjust your bindings.

Hooded jackets are popular. Jacket openings should seal tightly, and jackets should be vented, with side zippers that can be opened to release excess heat. Pants need extra padding at the hips and knees, and pants should have zippered vents also.

Wool sweaters are recommended because wool is warm and breathable. Instead of trapping your sweat, it draws it away from your body. Gloves or mitts should also be layered, with a waterproof outer covering and breathable interior layers.

The most common snowboarding injury is a sprained wrist, and wrist guards will prevent such injuries. Knee pads and a butt pad help cushion falls. Ski goggles will protect your eyes from the sun's rays and harsh winds or flying snow. Use sunscreen to protect your skin. You may need to apply sunscreen several times during the day.

To carry your board, bindings, boots, and everything else you need, you can get a snowboarding sack or bag. They come with both handle straps or an adjustable shoulder strap.

*Your outer layer should be waterproof, windproof, and also breathable. Martina Happ is pictured.*

# 6. SOME BASICS

*ARE YOU REGULAR OR GOOFY?"* That's the first question you'll be asked at a snowboarding school.

A "regular" rider has his or her left foot forward on the board. Those who are "goofy" lead with the right foot. About 70 percent of the population is regular. (It has nothing to do with whether you are right-handed or left-handed.)

It's easy to find out whether you are regular or goofy. Simply run in your socks for a few steps, then slide on a smooth floor. The foot you naturally lead with is the foot that should be placed forward on the board. (The instructions in this book are for a regular rider.)

For your first attempts at snowboarding, pick out a flat area with loosely packed snow or a few inches of powder.

For each of the exercises that follow, strap only your front foot into the binding. Strap in the ankle first, then the toes. Also hook up the safety strap. Your back foot is free. The purpose of these exercises is to help you develop the balance, control, and edging skills you need for downhill riding.

Stand erect, with your free foot beside the board in the snow. Pick up the front foot and swing the board back and forth. Swing the tip to the left and right. Keep repeating this drill until you get used to the weight of the board and the idea of having one foot turned inward so much.

Next, practice what's called skating. Push off with your free foot and slide the board forward. Keep your weight over your front foot. Keep repeating the drill: step and slide, step and slide.

*Skating is a simple step-and-glide maneuver.*

Skating is sure to feel very awkward at first. After all, your front foot is positioned across the board, with the toes pointing toward your free foot.

Take small steps at first, keeping the free foot close to the board. This helps prevent the board from swerving left or right.

After you've skated 30 or 40 feet, stop, then turn yourself around so as to face in the opposite direction. Do this in stages. With your weight on your free foot, swivel the board's tip to the left. Stop, move your free foot, and swivel the tip some more. Keep adjusting and swiveling until the board's tip is facing in the other direction. Then skate in that direction.

Next, try gliding. Build up some speed by skating. As the board slides, place your free foot on the deck mat. Bend your knees and extend your arms for balance. Look straight ahead.

Practice edging, too. The snowboard has two edges — the toe edge and the heel edge. With both feet in the bindings, roll forward onto the balls of your feet. This presses the board's toe edge into the snow.

Also practice rolling your weight onto your heels. This presses the heel edge into the snow.

Edging is a vital skill in snowboarding. Using your toes and heels, you pressure the board's edges to change direction and turn.

# 7. SIDESLIPPING

SIDESLIPPING, a maneuver in which you slide down the slope with the board at right angles to the fall line, will help you improve your balance and teach you the basics of edge control. (The fall line is the straightest and steepest line of descent down the slope, the path a ball would take if you released it at the top.)

Remember, sideslipping is a drill, a training exercise. It's not something you're going to be doing as an advanced rider.

For the exercises in this section and those that follow, pick out a long and gentle slope. "Gentle" is the key word. At mountain resorts, they're called bunny hills. For a beginner, a steep hill can be a source of danger.

Before you go down, you have to go up. Walking to the top requires that you have only your front foot in the binding.

Begin your trip up the hill by placing the board across the fall line, that is, at right angles to it. Facing uphill, roll onto your toes so as to press the board's toe edge into the snow. Once the toe edge is anchored, lift your free foot, cross it over the board, and plant it in the snow.

Then lift and drag the board up the hill step by step. It's going to feel very awkward at first. To feel less awkward, remember to take a big step with your free foot and a little step with the board.

Keep repeating the maneuver. Roll onto the toe edge, step uphill with your free foot, plant it, then lift the board up the hill. It isn't very speedy, but it works.

At the top of the slope, sit down and strap your free foot into the binding. Then try a sideslip from the heel-side first.

*In walking uphill, keep the board at right angles to the fall line.*

From a sitting position, face downhill with your board at right angles to the fall line. Stand up, pressuring the heel edge into the snow. You'll be balanced over the board's heel edge.

Release some of the heel-edge pressure and you'll start sideslipping down the slope. Keep yourself evenly balanced on both feet, your knees slightly bent.

You won't go very fast because the board is traveling sideways. If you do pick up speed and want to slow down or stop, simply rock back on your heels.

Never allow the board to ride flat on the snow. Do that and the other edge, the toe edge, may dig into the snow, throwing you forward. This is known as "catching an edge."

Next, try a toe-side sideslip, a maneuver in which you slide down the hill backwards.

At the top of the slope, face uphill, kneeling in the snow, the board behind you across the fall line. Then slowly get to your feet, pressuring the toe edge into the snow. You won't slide backward as long as you keep pressure on the toe edge.

To begin sideslipping, straighten your knees to release some of the toe-edge pressure. Since you're going downhill backwards, you have a vision problem — you can't see where you're going. Turn your head and look over your shoulder. To halt your slide, simply increase the toe-edge pressure

*In executing a heel-side sideslip, tilt back, putting pressure on the board's heel edge. Release some of the pressure and you start sideslipping.*

*In the toe-side sideslip, you face uphill, putting pressure on the toe edge. Reduce the edge pressure and the board starts to slide.*

As you become more skilled, increase the distance of your sideslips. Make each as smooth as possible. Be careful about catching edges.

Practice both the heel and toe sideslips. Practice until it becomes easy for you to control your speed and to stop.

# 8. TRAVERSING

*WHEN YOU PLUNGE* straight down a slope at top speed, you're following the fall line. When you begin to angle the nose of your board to the right or left across the fall line, you're riding on a slant, on a diagonal. That's traversing.

Traversing slows you down, enabling you to control the speed of your downhill runs. Once you're skilled at sideslipping, traversing should be easy to learn.

Try traversing from the heel-side first. Face downhill with the board at right angles to the fall line (as if you were about to perform a heel sideslip). Pressure the board's heel edge, which is also the uphill edge, into the snow.

Shift some of your weight to your back foot and pivot the nose of the board in a downward direction. You'll begin heading diagonally to your left; you'll be traversing. As you travel, you'll be riding on the board's heel edge, the uphill edge.

When you've traveled as far as you can and you want to stop, nose the board into more of an uphill direction. Roll onto your heels, increasing the pressure on the heel edge. If you've been traveling at a good amount of speed, you'll come to an abrupt stop, a dramatic stop. It's almost like a hockey stop in ice skating.

Once you're skilled in executing a heel-side traverse, try a traverse from the other side, the toe side.

Begin from a toe-side sideslip. You're facing

A heel-side traverse. Ride on the heel edge, traveling diagonally across the slope. To stop, increase the edge pressure and nose the board in the uphill direction.

uphill, with the board at right angles to the fall line. Press the board's toe edge, the uphill edge, into the snow.

Shift your weight onto your back foot and angle the nose of the board into a downhill direction.

*A toe-side traverse. Ride on the toe edge, increase the edge pressure and turn into the hill to slow down or stop.*

you're always traveling on one edge or the other. You're never riding flat-footed, never riding with the board flat to the snow. You're always applying pressure with your toes or your heels.

One other point: A failing some beginners have at this stage is looking down at the board and their feet as they travel. That can lead to disaster. Keep you chin up; focus on where you're going. Otherwise, you can run into a rock, a tree, another boarder, or some other obstacle. Always concentrate on the road ahead.

Again, control your speed by controlling the angle at which you're traveling.

You'll be traversing to the right.

To stop, nose the board straight across the fall line and into an uphill direction, increasing the toe-edge pressure.

It's important to remember that as you traverse

# 9. TURNING

*IN SNOWBOARDING*, there are two ways to turn: heel-side and toe-side. Try your first turns on a beginner's slope or at the end of a downhill run.

A heel-side turn is executed on the board's heel-edge side, and is a left turn. A toe-side turn is performed on the toe edge, and is a right turn.

To begin a heel side turn, look over your shoulder in the direction you want to turn, that is, to the left. Shift your weight onto your front foot. Roll onto the board's heel edge.

As the board begins to change direction, bend your knees slightly, then gently pivot the board around with your back leg. The board will cut across the fall line and head diagonally in the new direction.

Keep your weight evenly distributed as you continue your run. To stop, simply turn uphill.

To execute a toe-side turn, a turn to the right, begin by looking in the direction you want to turn. Shift your weight onto your front foot and roll onto the board's toe-side edge. Use your back leg to pivot the board around.

Never lean into a turn. Instead, it's a matter of first turning your head and body into the direction you want to go, while keeping erect over the board. As you cross the fall line, steer the board by pressing your back leg in a downhill direction. Keep practicing until you can steer the board smoothly through both heel-side and toe-side turns.

*For a heel-side turn, first look in the direction you want to turn. Roll onto the board's heel edge, then pivot the board through the turn with your back leg.*

The next step is to execute a series of turns as you make your way down a slope. After a series of turns, look back up the hill and you'll see that you've traced a series of S's in the snow.

Learning to turn, and doing it smoothly from beginning to end, is no easy matter. It takes practice and patience. Don't expect to become skilled in the art right away.

In executing a toe-side turn, look to your right, the direction of the turn. Rock onto the board's toe edge, then steer the board around with your back leg.

# 10. CARVING TURNS

*CARVED TURNS* are every rider's goal. Smoother and more elegant than skidded turns, they trace neater and narrower tracks in the snow, earning you oohs and aahs from your friends.

With skidded turns, the board skims along the snow's surface. But with carved turns you rely more on flexibility and sidecut to cause the board's edges to slide through the snow. Carved turns not only look great, they feel great.

As with any turns, carved turns are made on the heel-side edge or the toe-side edge. but you have

*With a carved turn, you shift pressure from one edge to the other; the board does the rest.*

to be aggressive; you have to really drive the knees forward. In so doing, you cause the board to tilt onto the edge and sweep into the arc of the turn.

Rise fast as you come out of the turn. Look in the direction you want to go.

Carved turns not only look better and feel better, they also sound better. Instead of the rasping, scraping sound you get with skidded turns, carved turns create a delicate whoosh. Every time you go out onto the slopes, you'll want to carve your turns.

*Not only are they smooth and graceful, carved turns are tighter turns. Burton team rider Peter Bauer demonstrates.*

# 11. FREESTYLE TRICKS

SNOWBOARDERS are divided into two categories. There are freestylers, boarders who focus on ground tricks and air tricks, such maneuvers as wheelies, spins, and grabs. Halfpipes and snowboard parks have been created for freestylers.

Alpine boarders make up the other category. Alpine boarders prefer riding fast down a mountain, carving as they go.

You've probably seen videos that feature freestyle tricks on MTV or ESPN. As you can judge, you've got to be really skilled and experienced before you try such antics. They're not for beginners.

Specialists in freestyle use boards that are "softer" than normal, that are more flexible, and thus easier to maneuver. And their boards are twin-tipped,

so they can be ridden backward as easily as forward.

There are countless tricks that can be performed on a snowboard. Some of the best known are described in this section.

Riding fakie — riding a snowboard backwards — is a common trick. Once you've mastered edge control, you can try riding fakie. As you come into a turn, instead of steering through it, you spin the board around a full 180° so that it's traveling tail first. What was once your front foot has become your rear foot, and vice versa. It looks a little weird. It feels weird, too.

Ground spins are also seen frequently. You've probably spun several times—accidentally. To exe-

*Air tricks can be awesome.*

cute a full 360° spin, start with a toe-side or heel-side turn, and keep going. As you approach 180°, it's likely that you'll begin slowing down. That's when you should flatten out your board and push your front foot hard in the direction of the spin. There are air spins, too, in which experienced

*Burton's Aleksi Vanninen demonstrates a side grab.*

boarders rocket into the air and then whirl about like a helicopter blade.

When you do a wheelie with your bike, you brake sharply, lift the front wheel in the air and balance on the rear wheel. A wheelie in snowboarding is similar. You lean way back, concentrating your weight on your rear foot, then pull up the board's nose. The longer you hold it up, the more spectacular the trick. Experts are also able to execute tip wheelies, lifting the board's tail.

If you've ever watched snowboarding videos, you've seen ollies. In performing an ollie, you crouch down, then leap up, using the tail of the board to spring high into the air. Once airborne, you level the board by bringing your knees to your chest, then land on both feet.

Grabs are also seen frequently. They're just what the name suggests. You reach down and grab hold of the board with one hand. There are tail grabs, toe grabs, and side grabs.

These are some of the standard snowboard tricks. It would take a book at least the size of this one to describe them all, and new ones are being invented every day. Snowboarding encourages creativity.

# 12. HALFPIPE TRICKS

*THE HALFPIPE,* a long steep-sided, specially constructed trench in the snow, shaped like a wide-based U, opens the door to exciting fun. Virtually any mountain resort that welcomes snowboarders has one.

The halfpipe has three parts: the flat, the two walls, and the transitions. The flat is the pipe's center floor and the walls are its sides, its vertical sections. In between the two are the transitions, called trannies, the ramplike sections that lead you from the flat onto the walls and beyond.

Most halfpipes also have what is known as a deck or platform. It is the flat surface beyond the top of the wall (known as the lip). The deck is your landing area should you zoom over the lip.

According to specifications set by the U. S. Ski Association (USSA), the halfpipe's walls should be 2 meters (6.5 feet) in height and there should be a distance of 15 meters (49.2 feet) between them. The structure should be 100 meters (328 feet) long. Although halfpipes differ from one ski area to the next, many are pretty close to these specifications.

The first time you ride a halfpipe, take it easy. Don't try any fancy tricks. Most boarders start with simple traverses. Ride to the top of one wall, pause, then turn and execute a traverse toward the opposite wall.

As you near the top of the wall opposite, get set to turn again. Execute the turn, riding on the opposite edge down the wall. You should always approach a wall on one edge, and leave it on the

*Halfpipe instruction at High Cascade Snowboard Camp.*

other. Once you become skilled, you can trace big U's up and down the walls. And you can go higher and higher.

If you're like most boarders, your ultimate goal will be to soar high above the wall, to "catch air," that is. A maneuver called the bunny hop will introduce you to the art of "catching air." As you near the top of the wall, concentrate on the lip. Lift your front foot slightly and add a little spring to your ride before you turn, a little bounce to get you airborne. Look back into the pipe and pick out the spot where you want to land. When your head turns, your body will follow. As you come down (on a new edge), absorb the impact with your knees.

Little by little, increase the distance of your hops. After a time, you won't be bunny hopping any more, you'll be catching air.

The halfpipe is only one of several custom-built challenges that some ski areas offer. There are also ramps, rails, spines, and table tops, all arranged imaginatively in a special area known as a snowboard park.

David Olcott of Morristown, New Jersey, is a designer of snowboard parks for major ski areas. At Waterville, New Hampshire, Olcott helped design a ten-acre snowboard park using mostly junkyard scrap. The sawed-off top of a school bus is the park's prize test. Snowboarders ride the roof, careening down the metal surface.

At Sugarbush, Vermont, there are two snowboard parks. For beginner to intermediate boarders, there's Phred, a four-acre layout. For more advanced riders, Sugarbush offers Fat Bob, a seven-acre park.

*Riding a rail at a snowboard park.*

# 13. ALL ABOUT SNOW

*ONCE YOU'RE SKILLED* and somewhat experienced as a boarder, you'll begin paying more and more attention to the snow conditions you're going to encounter. While the basic snowboarding techniques are the same no matter what type of snow covers the slopes, some slight changes in technique can be necessary.

Many experienced boarders prefer powdery snow. Boarding in light, dry, fluffy powder provides the ultimate in thrills and excitement. You're surfing; you're floating!

The key to boarding success in powder, whether it's natural or machine-made, is speed. You must go fast. If you slow down, you sink.

Speed allows you to glide through the snow, the way a water skier planes across a lake.

Besides generating plenty of speed, it's a good idea to keep your weight back more than usual. This keeps the tip up, encouraging the board to surf, to plane.

When changing direction in powder, be sure to maintain your speed; don't stall. It doesn't take great effort to turn in powder. Toe-side or heel-side, you only have to tilt the board slightly to change direction.

Unfortunately, powder isn't encountered very often in most parts of the country. Much more common is packed powder, loose powder that's been compacted by boarders and skier traffic or by mechanical means, that is, snow-grooming equipment. It's not hard to get the board to hold an edge when riding on packed powder. Controlling speed and turning are not difficult.

When powder thaws and then refreezes, loose granular snow is sometimes the result. This makes for a fast surface. It's hard to hold an edge. Be especially careful when riding on loose granular.

Frozen granular is even more of a hazard. This is wet snow that has frozen, forming a crusty surface. You have to work hard to control your speed on frozen granular.

Wet snow is just what the name suggests, snow that is moist and sticky as it falls. Snowballs are easy to make, but wet snow is a problem for boarders. It's difficult to generate real speed, to turn and maneuver.

There's also corn snow, common to the mountain ski resorts of the Northeast in the spring. Corn snow is produced over a series of days in which the snow thaws in the spring sun, then refreezes at night. Frozen granules the size of kernels of corn are the result. Boarding in corn snow, with the temperature about freezing, can be enjoyable. Speed is easy to control.

Most ski areas use these terms when reporting snow conditions. Before you set out on a day of boarding, check to see what type of snow you're going to encounter.

*When riding on light, dry powder, you must travel fast.*

# 14. SKI AREA RIDING

*IT WASN'T VERY LONG AGO* that snowboards were banned from most of the nation's ski areas. It wasn't until 1989, in fact, that such well-known resorts as Vail (Colorado), Squaw Valley (California), and Sun Valley (Idaho) began to welcome boarders.

It's much different today, of course. Of the 524 ski areas in the United States, according to a recent survey, 509 are ready to greet snowboarders.

The usual mountain resort is made up of one or more lodges, where you find rental shops, instruction schools, lift-ticket counters, snack bars, and restaurants. Close to the lodges are the bunny slopes and trails for beginners. Intermediate, advanced, and expert trails are higher up the mountain. Trail signs indicate how to reach each trail and indicate the degree of difficulty of each.

All major trails are serviced by lifts. There's a knack to riding lifts. After all, lifts were designed especially for skiers, which makes them a little bit tricky for boarders. Watch how other boarders ride a lift before you try. If you are taking a lift for the first time, tell the operator. He or she may give you a few tips or even slow down the lift so you can board more easily.

You usually have to wait in line for a lift. While waiting, keep only your front foot in the binding. Skate along as the line moves.

Most ski areas have chair lifts. When the chair lift approaches, reach out and grasp the chair support. Sit down quickly and slide way back into the seat. Be sure to keep your board pointing straight ahead. When you near the top, inch forward in the chair. Keep your weight on your front foot, with

*Above: As you ease into the chair lift, be sure to keep the tip of the board pointed straight ahead.*

*Right: In getting off the chair lift, use the seat edge to push yourself forward. Glide or skate away.*

the back foot on the deck mat. Again, be sure the board is pointed straight ahead. Push off from the front edge of the seat as the board hits the snow. Bend your knees. Glide down the unloading ramp and skate away from the unloading area.

There are other kinds of lifts, and some present more problems for boarders than others. In a gondola, or any type of enclosed lift, where do you put your board? Some have outside racks for boards, but most don't. You  have to take the board inside with you. Be careful to keep the tip and sharp edges away from other passengers.

Every mountain resort has its own type of lift. Find out ahead of time how best to use it. Every resort also has its own set of safety rules. Be sure to become aware of those rules and respect them.

# 15. SAFETY TIPS

WHEN YOU'RE OUT on a mountain for a day of snowboarding, nobody is going to be looking over your shoulder giving you advice. You're on your own, responsible for your own safety. Follow these rules:

1. Never ride alone. Be sure you're able to see and hear other riders.
2. Nothing is more embarrassing than a board that gets loose and dives downhill on its own. Use a strap or other device to prevent your board from getting away from you.
3. Always plan your descent from beginning to end. Actually visualize every foot of the run.
4. Always keep in control, able to change direction or stop to avoid other riders or skiers.
5. Before you cut across a trail or slope, look uphill and to each side. As a regular rider, be especially cautious when turning to the left. You're usually facing to the right as you ride, and may not have any idea what's happening off to your left. Be sure to check.
6. People ahead of you on a trail or slope have the right of way. It's your responsibility to avoid them.
7. On a slope, should you fall, get up quickly. Don't become a hazard.
8. Should you stop to adjust your bindings, move to the side of the trail or slope.
9. Observe all posted signs and warnings.

# GLOSSARY

**alpine** — A style of snowboarding that stresses speed and carved turns.

**alpine snowboard** — A stiffer than normal snowboard meant to maximize speed and hold an edge during turns.

**binding** — The fastening device that holds the boot to the board.

**carved turn** — A turn with no skid that relies on the board's flexibility and sidecut to change direction.

**catch air** — To soar beyond a halfpipe's upper edge or lip.

**catch an edge** — To mistakenly permit one of the board's edges to dig into the snow; catching an edge usually results in a spill.

**corn snow** — A condition that results when the snow surface keeps melting and refreezing, resulting in the formation of frozen granules that are about the size of corn kernels.

**deck mat** — The nonskid pad fixed to the snowboard between the bindings.

**edges** — The metal strips that run the length of the board on both sides of the base.

**fakie** — Riding backward.

**fall line** — The straightest and steepest line down a slope.

**flat** — In a halfpipe, the center floor.

**freestyle** — A style of snowboarding involving ground and air tricks and such maneuvers as spins and grabs.

**freestyle/freeride snowboard** — A board that is more flexible than average, with an identical nose and tail to enable the boarder to ride backward as well as forward.

**frozen granular** — Wet snow that has frozen so as to form a crusty surface.

**goofy** — A snowboarder who rides with his or her right foot forward on the board.

**halfpipe** — A U-shaped channel constructed in the snow, up to 328 feet long, with walls 5- to 10-feet high on each side.

**lip** — The top edge of the wall of a halfpipe.

**loose granular** — A type of snow that can result when powder thaws and refreezes.

**nose** — The snowboard's front tip.

**packed powder** — Light, dry snow that has been compacted by boarders, skiers, or mechanical equipment.

**powder** — Light, dry, fluffy snow.

**safety strap** — The strap used to fasten a snowboarder's front leg to the board so as to prevent a runaway board.

**sidecut** — A characteristic of a snowboard in which the tip and tail are wider than the waist.

**skating** — To advance the snowboard with only the front foot in its binding, pushing with the back foot.

**skidded turn** — A turn that relies on foot and leg pressure in changing direction, which causes the board to skim over the snow's surface.

**sideslipping** — Allowing the board to slide down the hill while at right angles to the fall line.

**tail** — The snowboard's back end.

**transition** — In a halfpipe, the ramplike section between the flat and the walls.

**traverse** — To ride diagonally across a hill.

**wet snow** — Snow that is moist and sticky as it falls.

# *FOR MORE INFORMATION*

## THE INTERNET

The World Wide Web offers wide information about snowboarding, some of it useful, some of it entertaining. Here, at the time of this book's publication, were two of the many addresses that dealt with the sport:
http://www.hyperski.com
http://www.airwalk.com/snow/snowriders.html

## VIDEOS

*Boarding School;* basic instruction presented in an entertaining manner, 30 minutes, ETC films.
*Starting From Scratch;* meant for women, ten easy steps for learning to ride, 30 minutes, Frontline Video & Film.
*Snowboarding, Tweaked and Twisted;* top pros ride halfpipes of Japan and the U.S. and surf Canadian powder, 46 minutes, a Warren Miller Production, Columbia Tristar Home Video.

## MAGAZINES

*Transworld Snowboarding*
353 Airport Rd.
Oceanside, CA 92054

*Snowboarder*
Surfer Publications, Inc.
33046 Calle Aviador
San Juan Capistrano, CA 92675

## ORGANIZATIONS

United States Ski Association Snowboarding
P.O. Box 100
Park City, UT 84060

United States Amateur Snowboarding Association
P.O. Box 4400
Frisco, CO 80443

Professional Snowboarders Association of North America
P.O. Box 477
Vail, CO 81658

International Snowboard Federation
P.O. Box 477
Vail, CO 81658

Canadian Snowboard Federation
1507 West 12th Avenue, Suite 30
Vancouver, British Columbia
Canada V6J 2E2